LITTLE KIDS
FIRST
BIG
BOOK OF
PETS

Catherine D. Hughes

NATIONAL
GEOGRAPHIC
KiDS

WASHINGTON, D.C.

CONTENTS

INTRODUCTION

This book introduces readers to pets. It answers questions from "Which animals make good pets?" and "What should I teach my puppy?" to "How do rabbits show excitement?" and "Why do cats sometimes rub people's legs?" After learning about the difference between the kinds of animals that make good pets and those that do not, readers explore popular pet animals throughout the rest of the book.

CHAPTER ONE begins the book with a look at what makes an animal wild, tame, domestic, stray, feral, or livestock. This helps identify which kinds of animals make the perfect pet. Readers find out where to find a pet to adopt or buy, and they discover how veterinarians play an important role in taking good care of pets. A fun photo game wraps up this and every other chapter, reinforcing topics covered in each section.

CHAPTER TWO is all about a very familiar pet: the dog. Starting off with playful puppies, the chapter covers purebreds and mutts. It features a gallery of working dogs and a diagram of basic dog anatomy. Play, communication, and training are all explained in the context of how to take good care of a pet pup.

CHAPTER THREE covers cats. From cuddling cute kittens to training cats, this chapter mirrors the topics explored for dogs, with unique feline features throughout.

CHAPTER FOUR introduces some small furry pets: rabbits, guinea pigs, hamsters, rats, mice, gerbils, and ferrets. One of our favorite pets to ride—the horse—wraps up this chapter.

CHAPTER FIVE starts with a look at pet birds, including cockatiels, budgerigars, lovebirds, and a few other charmers. Reptiles and amphibians, including snakes, lizards, turtles, and frogs, take the stage next. Hermit crabs offer an interesting perspective on what makes a good pet, followed by goldfish, bettas, and other finny friends.

HOW TO USE THIS BOOK

FACT BOXES highlight basic needs for the pet featured.

COLORFUL PHOTOGRAPHS illustrate each spread and support the text. Galleries showcase different breeds or species of the featured pets within the chapter.

HERMIT CRABS

Digging in sand and climbing rocks is all the exercise a hermit crab needs. This little creature is a crustacean, a group of animals that includes crabs and lobsters. A hermit crab is an easy pet to take care of—and fun to watch. Set up a terrarium, or clear glass tank, with sand, rocks, freshwater and salt water, and hiding places. Then add a couple of hermit crabs and let the fun begin!

Hermit crabs use abandoned snail shells for shelter. They carry their shells wherever they go. As they grow, they search for

BASIC NEEDS

hermit crab pellets

freshwater

salt water (made with special aquarium salt, not table salt)

fresh fruit and vegetables as a treat

terrarium with a warm temperature of about 75°F (24°C)

rocks and sand

daily misting with water to keep terrarium humid

places to hide and climb

new, larger shells for growing pet

112

What are some new things that you need as you grow bigger?

A hermit crab has **FIVE PAIRS OF LEGS.** It uses two pairs for walking, one pair for eating and climbing, one pair for fighting and climbing, and one pair to hold on to its shell.

FEATHERS AND SCALES

Hermit **CRABS** can go a **WEEK WITHOUT EATING.**

To pick up your **PET CRAB,** hold its shell in one hand and place its legs on the **FLAT PALM** of your other hand. He is less likely to pinch this way.

larger shells to use. When they find the right size, they crawl from the small shell to the bigger one and make themselves at home. If you have a pet hermit crab, you'll need to provide it with bigger and bigger shells as it grows.

113

INTERACTIVE QUESTIONS in each section encourage conversation related to the topic.

POP-UP FACTS sprinkled throughout provide added information and build on the main text in each section.

MORE FOR PARENTS in the back of the book offers parent tips that include fun activities that relate to pets, additional resources, and a helpful glossary.

A **GAME** at the end of each chapter reinforces concepts covered in that section.

CHAPTER 1
FAMILY PETS

A pet might be furry or covered in feathers, have four legs
or no legs. It might fit in your pocket or carry you on its back.
There are many kinds of pets, each with its own special way
to add fun to your family.

WHAT IS A PET?

A pet is an animal that lives with people and keeps them company. Cats and dogs are the most popular pets in the United States. Fish, guinea pigs, some kinds of birds, and rabbits are also popular. People enjoy pets for many reasons. Pets can be funny, playful, cute, cuddly, and smart. Scientists say that spending time with pets can help people feel happy, calm, and less lonely.

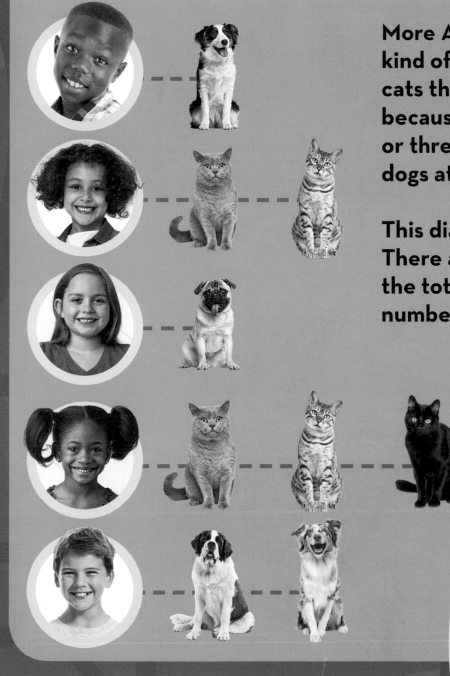

More Americans have dogs than any other kind of pet. However, there are more pet cats than pet dogs. How can that be? It is because a person is more likely to have two or three cats at a time than two or three dogs at a time.

This diagram helps explain this pet puzzle. There are five people who have pets. Count the total number of cats. Then count the number of dogs. Which number is higher?

How does it make you feel when you play with a dog, cat, or other pet?

WHAT IS NOT A PET?

People love wolves and penguins, tigers and elephants, deer and oxes, but none of them would make a good pet. They are wild animals.

Wild animals live outside and do not need people to take care of them. They would not be happy as pets, and they would be dangerous to keep in a home.

Can you name some wild animals that you have seen?

NEAR EASTERN WILDCATS are the **WILD ANCESTORS** of all **PET CATS.**

WOLVES are the **WILD ANCESTORS** of all **PET DOGS.**

A tame animal is a wild animal that has gotten used to being around people. A squirrel, for example, is a wild animal. But squirrels in parks and backyards often become unafraid of humans. They might come close to people. But even though a tame animal might look cute and cuddly, do not ever try to touch it. It is still wild, and it might bite or scratch you.

13

DOMESTICATED ANIMALS

Domesticated animals are those that have lived with humans for so long—over thousands of years—that they are no longer wild. Dogs and cats are domesticated animals. They need people to help take care of them. Domesticated animals make the best kinds of pets.

When people **FIND A STRAY ANIMAL,** they can take it to an **ANIMAL SHELTER.** The shelter workers try to find the stray's human family. If they cannot find its family, a new family may **ADOPT** it.

A stray animal is a domesticated animal that was a pet at one time, but for some reason began to live on its own. For example, a dog or cat that had a human family, but got lost, is a stray.

A feral animal is a domesticated animal that has never lived with humans. Feral animals are not friendly with people. They behave like wild animals. Feral cats, for example, live outdoors and catch mice and other small animals to eat.

Do you think it would be easier to be a feral cat or a pet cat? Why?

LIVESTOCK

Chickens, pigs, cows, sheep, goats, and other farm animals are called livestock. They are animals that ranchers and farmers raise mainly for food—milk, meat, and eggs. Sheep and some other kinds of livestock—alpacas and llamas—also provide wool. These animals are not usually considered to be pets.

A **PIG'S SQUEAL** can be almost as **LOUD** as a **JET'S ENGINE.**

Each day, a cow **DRINKS** about enough **WATER** to **FILL A BATHTUB.**

What kinds of livestock have you seen?

17

WHERE TO GET A PET

One great way to find a new pet is to visit an animal shelter. The people who work at animal shelters take care of dogs and cats that need homes and are waiting for someone to adopt them. They also take care of other pets that need homes, such as guinea pigs and rabbits.

More than **THREE MILLION PETS** are **ADOPTED** from shelters in the United States **EACH YEAR.**

Even if you can't **ADOPT A PET,** your family can **HELP ANIMALS** in shelters by donating **NEW TOYS, PET BEDS,** or **FOOD.**

If you could adopt a pet from an animal shelter, what kind would you most like to bring home?

Some pets come from a person called a breeder. A breeder provides specific kinds of pets called purebreds. You will find out more about purebreds later in the book.

PET STORE

GOLDEN RETRIEVERS have an average of **SEVEN PUPPIES** per litter.

A good breeder has just a few dogs, cats, or other kinds of pets. The breeder raises their babies to sell. People who buy these pets want a particular kind of animal.

Some pet stores sell a few kinds of pets. These stores also sell food, bedding, and other things pets need.

A group of **KITTENS** or **PUPPIES** born at the same time is called a litter.

Sometimes a person's cat, dog, or other pet has babies. People usually cannot keep all the baby animals, so they give them away or sell them to people who want a new pet.

21

DOCTORS FOR PETS

Kids usually have a special doctor called a pediatrician. That's a doctor who takes care of kids when they are sick or when they need a checkup. Pets have special doctors, too. They are called veterinarians. People take pets to veterinarians for the same reasons kids go to pediatricians.

Just like a **PEDIATRICIAN**, a vet uses a **STETHOSCOPE** to listen to your pet's **HEART** and **LUNGS.**

A veterinarian makes sure a pet is growing well and that everything in its body is working properly. She treats pets that are sick or injured. She gives pets vaccinations—medicine that prevents certain diseases—to help keep them healthy.

What do you like best about going to the pediatrician when you need a checkup?

VETERINARIANS ON THE GO

Most veterinarians work in a clinic. But some vets go to a family's home to give a pet a checkup or take care of a sick pet. They are called mobile vets. Mobile vets drive around from home to home, taking their equipment and medicine in their vehicle with them.

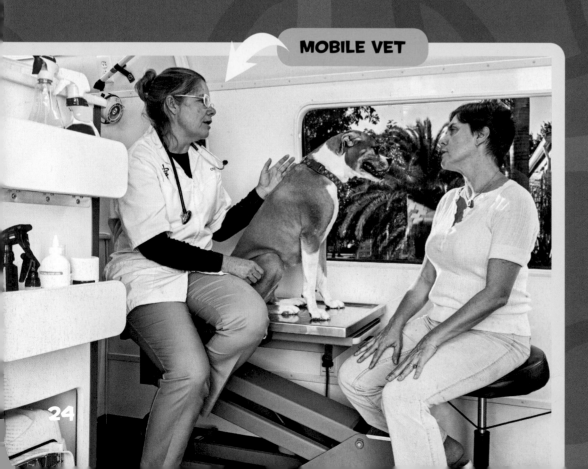

MOBILE VET

MOBILE VET VEHICLE

24

EQUINE VET

Would you rather be a doctor for people or pets? Why?

A veterinarian who specializes in caring for horses is called an equine vet. Horses are way too big to fit into a car to take to a vet clinic. So equine vets drive to wherever the horses are—on a farm, at a stable, or in a field—to take care of them.

LET'S PLAY A GAME!

Match each photo to the word that best describes the group of animals to which it belongs.

WILD

PET

LIVESTOCK

27

CHAPTER 2
DOGS

From tiny pups that could fit into your cereal bowl to giant dogs that would cover your whole bed, this chapter tells you about a popular pet that comes in many sizes, shapes, and personalities.

PUPPIES

BASIC NEEDS

- puppy food
- bowl of fresh, clean water
- collar with identification tag
- leash
- dog brush and comb
- warm, comfy dog bed
- dog toys

The day a family decides to get a puppy is so exciting! Puppies are bouncy, funny, fluffy little bundles of cuteness. Before a puppy is ready to join his new human family, however, he needs to stay with his doggy family for a while. He needs to nurse, or drink milk from his mother, for almost two months.

Puppies do not **OPEN THEIR EYES** until they are about **TWO WEEKS OLD.**

A **PUPPY SLEEPS** about **16 HOURS** every day.

Puppies learn from their mom, brothers, and sisters how to get along with others. They learn how to play without biting or hurting each other. Those lessons help make a puppy a good playmate for humans later on. A puppy is ready for adoption when he is about eight weeks old. By then he won't need his mother's milk and can just eat solid food.

TOOTHPASTE made for **DOGS** comes in **CHICKEN** and **PEANUT BUTTER** flavors.

How many hours do you usually sleep each night?

KINDS OF DOGS

Dogs are all one species, or kind, of animal—just like we humans are all one species. But just like humans, dogs can look very different from one another.

Tiny, short-haired Chihuahuas, for example, look very different from big, fluffy Old English sheepdogs. That's because Chihuahuas and sheepdogs are different breeds, or types, of dogs.

CHIHUAHUA

A dog that is just one breed is called a purebred. For example, a purebred Chihuahua has parents that are both Chihuahuas.

A mixed-breed dog, often called a mutt, is a dog made up of several breeds. For example, meet Moose. He is a lovable mutt mix of golden retriever, bloodhound, Jack Russell terrier, and a few other breeds!

MOOSE THE MUTT

The Labrador retriever, German shepherd, and golden retriever are the **THREE MOST POPULAR DOG BREEDS** in the United States.

CROSSBREED

cocker spaniel mommy + **poodle daddy** = **cockapoo puppy**

A crossbreed dog is one that has a mother that is one breed and a father that is another breed. A cockapoo, for instance, is a cross between a cocker spaniel and a poodle.

33

GIANT DOGS

An organization called the American Kennel Club (AKC) is an authority, or expert, on dog breeds. The AKC recognizes 192 breeds of dogs. Dogs range in size from huge to tiny. Here are the 10 largest dog breeds. The height is measured at the dogs' shoulders.

SIZE

This shows how big a Great Dane is. It is the tallest of all the dogs shown here.

GREAT DANE

FIVE-YEAR-OLD

GREAT DANE
34 inches (86 cm),
200 pounds (91 kg)

IRISH WOLFHOUND
32 inches (81 cm),
120 pounds (54 kg)

SCOTTISH DEERHOUND
32 inches (81 cm),
110 pounds (50 kg)

GREAT PYRENEES
32 inches (81 cm),
100 pounds (45 kg)

LEONBERGER
31.5 inches (80 cm),
170 pounds (77 kg)

NEAPOLITAN MASTIFF
31 inches (79 cm),
150 pounds (68 kg)

MASTIFF
30 inches (76 cm),
230 pounds (104 kg)

Dogs often **DREAM.** Sometimes they even **BARK** or **MOVE THEIR LEGS** while they're sleeping.

TIBETAN MASTIFF
30 inches (76 cm),
160 pounds (72.5 kg)

People used to train the Great Pyrenees to **GUARD LIVESTOCK** at night. This breed is still often **AWAKE AND ALERT** while its humans sleep!

BLACK RUSSIAN TERRIER
30 inches (76 cm),
130 pounds (59 kg)

NEWFOUNDLAND
28 inches (71 cm),
150 pounds (68 kg)

TINY DOGS

Some dogs are teeny-tiny! Here are 12 of the smallest dog breeds listed by the AKC. The height is measured at the dogs' shoulders.

SIZE

This shows how big a miniature dachshund is. It is the shortest of all the dogs shown here.

MINIATURE DACHSHUND

FIVE-YEAR-OLD

MINIATURE DACHSHUND
5 inches (13 cm),
11 pounds (5 kg)

POMERANIAN
6 inches (15 cm),
3 pounds (1.3 kg)

CHIHUAHUA
6 inches (15 cm),
3 pounds (1.3 kg)

PEKINGESE
6 inches (15 cm),
14 pounds (6.3 kg)

YORKSHIRE TERRIER
7 inches (18 cm),
7 pounds (3.1 kg)

BRUSSELS GRIFFON
7 inches (18 cm),
8 pounds (3.6 kg)

PAPILLON
8 inches (20 cm),
5 pounds (2.2 kg)

MALTESE
8 inches (20 cm),
6 pounds (2.7 kg)

JAPANESE CHIN
8 inches (20 cm),
7 pounds (3.1 kg)

"PAPILLON" means **"BUTTERFLY"** in French. The breed got its name because the **DOG'S EARS** fan out like a butterfly's wings.

SHIH TZU
8 inches (20 cm),
9 pounds (4 kg)

TOY FOX TERRIER
8.5 inches (22 cm),
3.5 pounds (1.6 kg)

HAVANESE
8.5 inches (22 cm),
7 pounds (3.1 kg)

PLAYTIME!

Chasing balls, playing hide-and-seek, splashing in a stream, racing around in a game of tag, leaping up to catch a Frisbee, pulling hard during a game of tug-of-war—these are all ways dogs play. Does that sound like how *you* like to play, too?

Playing with a pet dog is more than just fun. It also gives a pup the attention and exercise that all dogs need. Many dogs enjoy playing with other dogs.

Certain types of **BACTERIA** can make a **DOG'S PAWS SMELL LIKE POPCORN** or corn chips.

One good place for dogs to play together is at a fenced-in dog park. People can bring their pups, take off their dogs' leashes, and let them run around with the other dogs.

What is your favorite activity or game to play outdoors?

DOGGY PLAYGROUND

If a dog does these things at the dog park, it means it is playing happily:

- Leans down on its front legs with its rear up in the air
- Opens its mouth in what looks like a big grin
- Bounces around, acting goofy
- Falls over to show its belly when playing chase
- Goes back for more play

DOGS WITH JOBS

Some dogs have special jobs to do. But they don't work all the time. When they are done working for the day, they get to relax and play, just like other pets. Here are a few kinds of dogs with jobs.

DETECTION DOGS help sniff out trouble, often at airports. These dogs let an officer know if they smell something illegal inside a suitcase.

POLICE DOGS are trained to help police officers. These dogs help find lost kids, capture bad guys, and warn officers of trouble.

SERVICE DOGS help people with special needs. For example, a service dog might be trained to guide someone who is blind.

POLICE DOG

SERVICE DOG

THERAPY DOG

THERAPY DOGS

make people feel better. By visiting people in a hospital or in a nursing home, and snuggling and cuddling with them, these dogs help people who are sick or lonely feel happier.

MILITARY WORKING DOGS are similar to police and detection dogs. These pups help soldiers by alerting them to danger and by finding lost soldiers.

SEARCH AND RESCUE DOGS find people buried by snow in an avalanche or in buildings after an earthquake.

HERDING DOGS keep sheep or cattle moving wherever a rancher wants them to go.

Which of these dogs do you think has the hardest job? Why?

41

A DOG'S BODY

No matter what breed they are, all dogs have the same basic body parts.

EARS
Dogs hear a lot better than people do. A dog has 18 muscles in each of its ears that it can move around to catch sounds. You have six muscles in each of your ears.

TAIL
The way a dog holds its tail shows how it is feeling, such as happy or scared.

PAWS
Dogs have tough pads on their feet. Their pads are not as sensitive to cold, heat, and roughness as your bare feet are.

EYES
Dogs can see colors, but not as many as you probably can. Dogs cannot see things as far away as you can, either.

NOSE
Dogs can smell things thousands of times better than you can. A dog has about 300 million smell receptors, or receivers, in its nose, compared to your six million.

TONGUE
Dogs have only 1,700 taste buds on their tongue, compared to about 9,000 taste buds on your tongue. Dogs have special taste buds at the tip of their tongue that help them identify water.

TEETH
Dogs have more teeth than people. Puppies have 28 baby teeth. Human kids have 20. Adult dogs have 42 teeth. Adult humans have 32.

UNDERSTANDING YOUR DOG

Before you pet a dog you do not know, always **ASK ITS OWNER** whether it is okay. If the owner says that you may pet the dog, first put your hand out **SLOWLY, PALM DOWN,** and **LET THE DOG SNIFF** the back of your hand.

Dogs communicate with, or talk to, people in a bunch of ways. You have already read a little about dogs that want to play (pages 38–39), and what their tails say (page 42). Here are a few more ways a dog talks to you.

BARKING

If a dog barks really fast, and keeps it up, she is telling you that something is wrong. Arf, arf, arf! "Come quickly," the dog is saying. She might even be saying, "There is a fire in the kitchen!" So it is a good idea to go check and see why the dog is barking. Dogs have many other barks that sound different and that mean different things. Some dogs howl just for fun, as if they are singing!

BELLY-UP

"Please rub my belly" is what a dog lying on his back with his front legs bent is telling you.

BEGGING STARE

A dog that stares at someone who is sitting at the table eating is begging. "Please, please, please, give me a piece of that hamburger!" the dog's stare is saying. The best thing to do is to ignore her. Her dog food is much healthier for her than people food.

ANGRY DOG

Uh-oh. A dog with his ears up and his lips pulled back, teeth showing, is saying "Back off. Leave me alone." You should always leave an angry dog alone.

YAWNING

When you yawn, it usually means you are tired and sleepy. When a dog yawns, it means she is nervous or a bit upset. By yawning, the dog calms herself down and relaxes.

FULL-BODY SHAKE

A wet dog shakes himself to dry off, but sometimes a dog shakes when he is already dry. Why? When a dog becomes overexcited—maybe his best human friend just came home—he wiggles and jumps and barks with joy. He is so excited he can hardly stand it! If after all that, he still feels supercharged, the dog shakes his whole body to help himself calm down.

TRAINING A PUPPY

Training, or teaching, a puppy to behave and follow certain commands is very important. It is the best way to make sure that your pup stays safe and that your family enjoys her company.

Puppies can start training when they are about three or four months old. Here are five commands that all puppies should learn.

"Come!" is very important for a puppy to know and obey. If an excited pup runs toward a busy street, she needs to listen and obey when she hears "Come!"

Obeying could save her life—keeping her from getting hit by a car.

TRAINING PUPPIES should be done for only about **FIVE OR 10 MINUTES** at a time.

Some people take their puppies to **SPECIAL DOG-TRAINING CLASSES.** Others train their puppies themselves.

Every puppy should learn how to *"heel."* To heel means to walk by a person's side, without pulling at the leash.

"Sit" and *"Stay"* are two more useful commands. You might need the words when it is time for your puppy's dinner so she does not jump around and knock over her bowl.

The fifth command for your puppy to learn is *"Lie down."* This helps a pup know when it is dinnertime, bedtime, or just quiet time for her human family.

EVERYDAY CARE FOR A DOG

Each day, you need good food to eat, and plenty of water to drink. You need to go to the bathroom, and brush or comb your hair. You enjoy exercise and playtime. You get love and attention from your family. You need rest at times during the day, and at night, you need hours of sleep.

Guess what? A pet dog needs all of those things every day, too!

Dogs need dog food, not people food, to stay healthy. They need fresh water to drink. They need to be taken outside to pee and poop several times a day.

When you get bored, what do you do about it?

48

Not all dogs need to be **BRUSHED.** Why? Because some breeds, like this American hairless terrier, **DON'T HAVE ANY HAIR!**

Brushing a dog helps keep him clean and nice-looking. It also gets rid of loose fur, so your pup does not shed as much. Dogs usually do not need a bath more than a few times a year.

It is important for dogs to get plenty of exercise and play to keep them from getting bored. A bored dog can get into trouble—from chewing on things that could hurt him to barking too much.

Dogs take naps during the day and generally sleep through the night. They need a comfortable, warm, quiet spot for sleeping.

CHOOSING A DOG

Picking the right dog for your family takes some thought. For example, if you live in an apartment, you probably do not want a gigantic dog that needs a lot of room. Some kinds of dogs are known for being especially great friends for kids. If your family already has a pet, you will want a dog that gets along with other animals.

TEN POPULAR NAMES FOR FEMALE DOGS

Bailey • Bella
Daisy • Lola • Lucy
Luna • Maggie • Molly
Sadie • Sophie

TEN POPULAR NAMES FOR MALE DOGS

Bear • Buddy
Charlie • Cooper • Duke
Jack • Max • Oliver
Rocky • Tucker

At a shelter, the staff can help you find the right dog. If your family wants a purebred, you can check the AKC, which lists each breed with information about its personality.

If you were to get a new pup, what kind would you pick?

LET'S PLAY A GAME!

Use the pictures to help you read this story about a family who gets a new puppy.

A family drives to a shelter to pick out a .

The  read about  behavior before

they went to the shelter. They also made sure that they had

 , , a ,

a  , and a lot of  at home.

At the shelter, one cute female

asks for a belly rub. Then the wants to play.

The  name her Molly. They are excited to take her

home. is excited, too!

CHAPTER 3
CATS

Cats come in a variety of colors. They can be long-haired or short-haired. These fascinating, acrobatic athletes have been kept as pets since ancient times.

KITTENS

Mew, mew, mew! **Newborn kittens are mostly helpless, but they know how to find the milk from their mother's belly.** A mama cat nurses her hungry kittens. She feeds them often, keeps them clean by licking them, and cuddles them as they sleep.

During a little kitten's time with its cat family, it learns how to pee and poop in a litter box. It also learns how to be a nice kitty from its mother, brothers, and sisters—just as puppies do with their families.

"COPYCAT" is a term that comes from the way a kitten COPIES what its MOTHER does.

BASIC NEEDS

kitten food

bowl of fresh, clean water

litter box

cat brush and comb

warm, comfy cat bed

cat toys

scratching post or pad

safety cat collar and identification tag

As kittens play with each other, they learn not to hurt their playmates. Play bites are gentle. The kittens' sharp little claws mostly stay tucked away as they play. All these cat lessons make a kitten a wonderful pet by the time it goes home with its human family. Kittens are old enough to be adopted by a human family when they are about three months old.

Can you think of any ways that you are a copycat?

KINDS OF CATS

No matter how different cats may look, all of them are the same species of animal—just as all dogs are the same species. Also like dogs, there are many breeds of cats, as well as mixed breeds.

Cats come in many colors. They often have fun and interesting patterns, including mittens, mustaches, hearts, split-color faces, and more. Some cats have long hair, some have short hair, and a couple of breeds have no hair!

58

A cat with **THREE COLORS** of fur is called a **CALICO.** Usually a calico is mostly **WHITE,** with separate splotches of **BLACK** and **ORANGE.**

LONG-HAIRED CATS

The Cat Fanciers' Association (CFA) is an authority on cat breeds.
The CFA recognizes 42 breeds of cats. It describes cats by color, pattern, and length of the cat's hair. Here are some long-haired breeds.

BALINESE

TURKISH VAN

BIRMAN

RAGAMUFFIN

RAGDOLL

SIBERIAN

PERSIAN

SOMALI

LONG-HAIRED CATS need to be BRUSHED or COMBED more often than short-haired cats.

MAINE COON CAT

TURKISH ANGORA

NORWEGIAN FOREST CAT

If you had a ragamuffin cat, what would you name it?

SHORT-HAIRED CATS

Here are some short-haired breeds of cats.

ABYSSINIAN

AMERICAN WIREHAIR

BOMBAY

EGYPTIAN MAU

EUROPEAN BURMESE

OCICAT

CORNISH REX

DEVON REX

BURMESE

CHARTREUX

SIAMESE

SINGAPURA

HAIRLESS CAT

The sphynx is called the "hairless" cat, even though it is not completely hairless. It usually has a bit of hair around its nose, ears, toes, and tail. Its skin is loose and wrinkly.

SPHYNX

Would you rather have a long-haired or a short-haired cat? Why?

PLAYTIME!

Kittens and cats love to play. Many cat games use their hunting skills—stalking (sneaking up on things) and chasing.

When you play with a kitten or cat, use cat toys that the kitty can hold onto with her claws, such as a stuffed animal. Toss balls with bells inside for your cat to chase. Wiggle a stick with feathers on the end for her to leap at and catch.

Kittens and cats have sharp claws, so do not use your hands as toys when you play. You could get scratched. You want your cat to know that your hands are for petting and holding her, not for biting or scratching.

Some cats enjoy playing hide-and-seek. Others like to stalk things dragged across the floor, like a cloth measuring tape.

Can you think of other ways to play with a cat?

A CAT'S BODY

No matter what breed they are, all cats have the same basic body parts.

EARS
Cats can hear some sounds that humans—and others that even dogs—cannot hear. A cat can point its ears toward a soft sound, like a mouse scurrying by. It can even move each ear in a different direction from the other.

TAIL
A cat's tail helps the cat balance as it runs and turns.

PAWS
Cats have five toes on their front paws, and four on their back paws. Each toe has a claw. A cat can pull its claws into its toes or push them out. (Dogs' claws stay out.)

EYES
Cats see differently from the way you do. They can see farther to the sides without turning their heads. They can also see better in the dark than you can.

WHISKERS
The whiskers on a cat's face help it feel its way around in the dark. Whiskers also help a cat sense whether it can fit into a tight space.

NOSE
Cats can smell things about 14 times better than you can.

TONGUE
A cat can't taste as many things as you can. It has about 470 taste buds on its tongue. Your tongue has about 9,000. Like dogs, cats have special taste buds to sense water. A cat's tongue is rough. A kitty uses it like a brush to clean and comb its fur.

TEETH
Kittens have six more baby teeth than human kids do. But adult cats have two fewer teeth than adult people do.

67

UNDERSTANDING YOUR CAT

TWO CATS fighting make horrible, loud sounds called **CATER-WAULING.**

Meow! That is one way your cat talks to you, but it has a lot more to say. Check out these other ways kitties chat.

SOUNDS

Hiss! That is what a cat says to try to warn away something scary, like an unfriendly dog. Angry cats make a loud *yowl*. Cats meow at humans, but not usually to each other. Meowing can mean many things, from "I'm hungry" to "I need petting." When a cat purrs, it may be very happy. But cats also may purr when they are nervous or feel sick.

HEAD-BUTTS AND BODY RUBS

If a cat bonks its head on yours or rubs against your legs, it is probably letting you know that it likes you.

LICKING
Cats lick each other to show they like each other. Often after a person pets a cat, the cat licks back. It is a sign of affection.

BELLY-UP
When a kitty lies on its back and looks up at you, it is not asking for a belly rub the way a dog does. Cats do not like belly rubs. A cat doing this is just saying it trusts you. When a kitten rolls onto its back with another kitten, it is an invitation to play.

EARS HELD FLAT
If you see a cat with its ears turned and flattened against its head, watch out! It is either very scared, ready to fight, or both.

FLUFFED-OUT TAIL
If a cat is scared of something—maybe another cat that wants to fight—it may try to make itself look bigger. Its tail gets big and fluffy, and the cat holds it away from its body. This may make the other cat back off.

INSIDE OR OUTSIDE CAT?

Should a cat live inside only? Should it be allowed to go outside? The American Society for the Prevention of Cruelty to Animals (ASPCA) is an organization that recommends that pet cats be kept indoors. An outdoor cat faces dangers such as cars, coyotes that hunt small animals for food, dogs that might hurt cats, and even fights with other cats.

Some cat lovers do let their pets go outside. These owners need to keep a close eye on their cats. They need to make sure they come home to eat, and they need to keep their cats indoors in bad weather.

If you got a new kitten, what would you name a female? What would you name a male?

POPULAR NAMES FOR MALE CATS

Charlie
Jack • Jasper
Milo • Simon
Simba

POPULAR NAMES FOR FEMALE CATS

Bella • Chloe
Lily • Lucy
Luna • Molly

Most pet cats are perfectly happy staying inside. There are even some cats that enjoy walking on a leash. That is a great way to keep a kitty safe while still letting it visit the outdoors.

TRAINING A KITTEN

Kittens are tougher to train than puppies, but they can definitely learn a thing or two. The best way to train a kitten is to give him a special food treat and praise when he does the right thing.

A kitten can **LEARN TO SIT** on command, **PLAY FETCH** with **A BALL,** and come when **CALLED.**

Never punish him for doing the wrong thing. That just scares him; it does not teach him anything.

When you see your kitty using a scratching post, give him a treat and tell him how good he is. When your new kitty goes to the bathroom in the litter box, praise him and give him a treat so he knows he went in the right spot.

After a while, you can stop the treats and just give your cat a cuddle or praise when you see him doing the right thing.

What is the hardest thing you ever learned to do?

EVERYDAY CARE FOR A CAT

Like dogs, cats need food and water. They need exercise, play, love from family, rest, and nighttime sleep. But there is one thing a pet cat needs that a dog does not: a place to scratch.

A cat **GROOMS** itself several times a day, **LICKING** its fur to keep it clean.

Special scratching posts and pads will help keep her from scratching furniture and carpets.

A cat also needs a litter box, which is where she goes to the bathroom. Keeping the litter box clean is important. Cats will not use the litter box if it is too smelly.

Find a quiet, safe place for the cat's bed. She may sleep there, or she might pick her own comfy spot somewhere else.

A kitten is like a baby. She needs to be protected from things she should not play with. Put away small toys she could swallow. Make sure she does not chew on electrical cords.

DOGS AND CATS AS BUDDIES

Some dogs like to chase squirrels, birds—and cats. However, not all dogs chase cats, and not all cats scratch and hiss at dogs. They can be best friends. If a puppy and kitten are raised together, the friendship is an easy one. If they are introduced to each other when they are older, they might need some time to learn to get along.

CHOOSING A CAT

This **SHELTER CAT** with green eyes is waiting to be **ADOPTED!**

SCRATCHING POST

Picking the right cat for your family takes some thought. A playful kitten can get into a lot of mischief! It needs a family that is not too busy to give it a lot of time and attention. An older cat that is a bit less likely to get into trouble might be the right choice for another family.

Shelters have plenty of cats that are ready to be adopted. The shelter staff can point out special things about each cat. This will help you choose the best one for your family.

Some families want a particular breed of cat. Maybe a Siamese cat, a breed that tends to be very "talkative" and loving, is the right choice. Or maybe a quiet, fluffy Persian cat is just the right cat to pick.

If you were to get a new cat, what kind would you get?

The **SCOTTISH FOLD** is a breed of cat that can be long-haired or short-haired. Its **EARS ARE FOLDED** forward and down on its **HEAD.**

LET'S PLAY A GAME!

An animal shelter worker put pictures of her favorite eight cats on her office wall. Using the clues, can you figure out each cat's name?

CLUES

- Charlie is a popular Halloween cat.
- Bella could be a great pet for people who do not want a furry cat.
- Jasper is the color of both Charlie and Chloe.
- Luna has the pattern of a tiger.
- Milo has something in common with pumpkins, oranges, and tangerines.
- Molly is the color of Chloe, Charlie, and Milo.
- Simba is the color of many grandparents' hair.
- Chloe is hard to find in the snow.

A

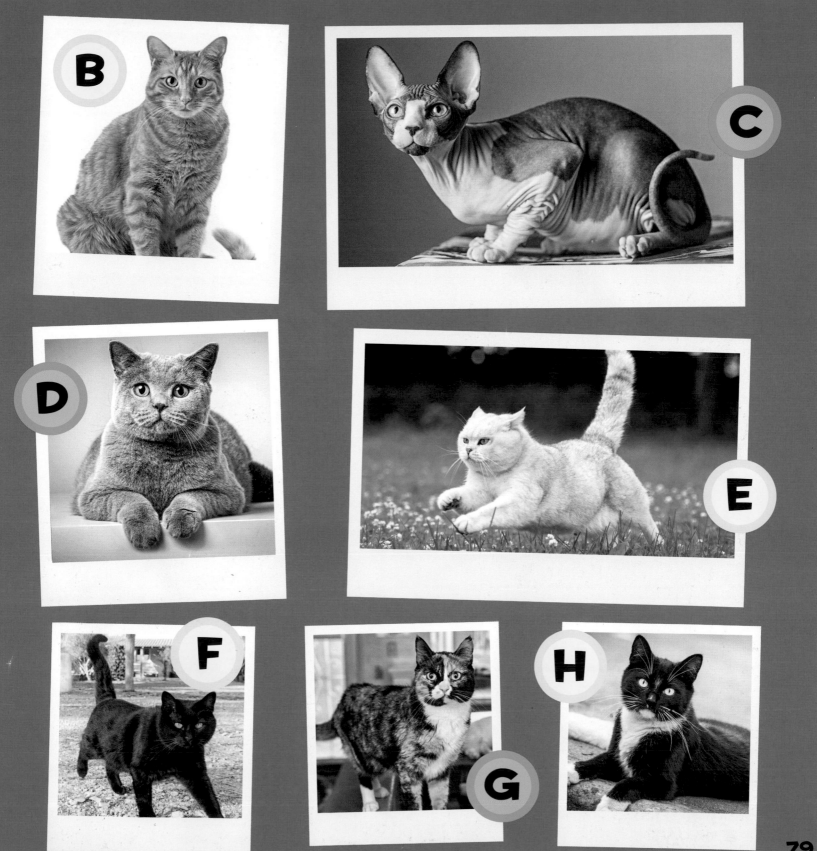

ANSWERS: A. LUNA; B. MILO; C. BELLA; D. SIMBA; E. CHLOE; F. CHARLIE; G. MOLLY; H. JASPER

CHAPTER 4
OTHER FURRY FRIENDS

You've read about dogs and cats. Now, from fuzzy little animals you can cuddle to big ones you can ride, this chapter introduces you to eight more pets.

RABBITS

A ball of fur leaps into the air! It twists its head in one direction while its body twists in the other. It's a rabbit doing a binky!

BASIC NEEDS

rabbit pellets and hay; fresh vegetables as a treat
....
fresh water
....
pen or cage
....
litter box and litter
....
rabbit toys

This crazy bunny dance lets you know that your pet rabbit is excited and happy. Pet rabbits enjoy playing with cardboard boxes and paper towel rolls, little balls with bells inside, and many toys made especially for rabbits.

PET RABBITS range in size from less than **3 POUNDS** (1 kg) to about **15 POUNDS** (6.8 kg).

A RABBIT DOING A BINKY

Most of all, your pet rabbit likes to play with you. Make plastic block towers for your bunny to knock over. He loves to nose-bonk! He will also enjoy grabbing a little plastic ball in his teeth and flinging it—especially if you go fetch it back for him.

BUNNY BREEDS

Pet rabbits come in many sizes and colors. Here are just a few breeds.

THRIANTA
4–6 pounds (1.8–2.7 kg)

A pet **RABBIT** likes to be where the **ACTION IS,** close to the company of his **HUMAN FAMILY.**

HIMALAYAN
2.5–5 pounds (1–2 kg)

FLORIDA WHITE
4–6 pounds (1.8–2.7 kg)

JAPANESE HARLEQUIN
6.5–9.5 pounds (2.9–4.3 kg)

CHINCHILLA
5.5–7 pounds (2.4–3.1 kg)

CALIFORNIAN
8–10.5 pounds (3.6–4.7 kg)

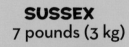

SUSSEX
7 pounds (3 kg)

DUTCH
4–5.5 pounds (1.8–2.2 kg)

FRENCH LOP
10–15 pounds (4.5–6.8 kg)

HAVANA
4.5–6.5 pounds (2–2.9 kg)

DOMESTICATED RABBITS are different from the **WILD RABBITS** you might see in a **GARDEN** or **PARK**.

GUINEA PIGS

BASIC NEEDS

guinea pig pellets, hay, fresh fruits and vegetables

water bottle

food dish

guinea pig cage

guinea pig bedding

chew toys

Purr. Whistle. Rumble. Squeal. Chirp. These are all guinea pig noises. When someone holds and pets it, a guinea pig might purr. If it is excited—such as when it is about to be fed—a guinea pig is likely to whistle.

When it is scared, a guinea pig makes a rumbling sound. Squealing means it might be hurting. A baby guinea pig sometimes chirps when it is hungry.

There are 13 breeds of guinea pigs, and they all come in a variety of colors. Some have short hair, and others have long hair. Here are a few breeds of guinea pigs.

Guinea pigs are **RODENTS**, a group of animals that includes **MICE** and **RATS**.

ABYSSINIAN GUINEA PIG

AMERICAN GUINEA PIG

SILKY SATIN GUINEA PIG

PERUVIAN GUINEA PIG

HAMSTERS

Like guinea pigs, **HAMSTERS** are **RODENTS.**

BASIC NEEDS

hamster pellets; fresh fruits, vegetables, and cheese as treats
....
clean water
....
hamster cage
....
hamster wheel for exercise and tubes for exploring
....
bedding and shredded paper or tissue

TEDDY BEAR HAMSTER

Unlike you, hamsters sleep during the day and are active during the night. The most common pet hamster is a breed called the teddy bear hamster. Teddy bear hamsters like to live alone, without any other hamsters.

The European hamster is the largest breed. It can grow to be as long as this page. The smallest breed is the dwarf hamster. It can fit in an adult's hand.

EUROPEAN HAMSTER

DWARF HAMSTER

Hamsters have **POCKETS** in their **CHEEKS** that they fill with food. They **BURY** the **FOOD** in their bedding to save for later.

Hamsters are easy to take care of. They make good, gentle pets. But they do sometimes bite, especially if they are scared or startled. When they are asleep, leave them alone! They tend to be grumpy if you wake them.

If you could have a pet rabbit, guinea pig, or hamster, which would you pick? Why?

RATS AND MICE

MOTHER rats usually have **12 BABIES** at a time, but sometimes have up to **20.**

RAT

Pet rats and mice are often called fancy rats and fancy mice. These fancy rodents are different from the rats and mice that live in sewers and scrounge around in garbage outdoors.

RATS and **MICE** are most **ACTIVE** at **NIGHT.**

MICE

RAT

Rats and mice are playful, acrobatic, and fun to watch. They are also good at escaping from cages. They destroy things they chew on, and they are naturally a bit smelly. They need a big cage, and they like to live with another rat (or mouse). Rats can be cuddly, but mice are usually squirmy.

91

GERBILS

GERBILS like COMPANY. One pet gerbil is likely to get LONELY, so it is better to have TWO.

Pet gerbils are usually awake when you are— during the day. They are fun to watch as they scurry around their cage, exercising on a spinning wheel, chewing on their food, and digging into their bedding. They are fast movers.

Gerbils can be hard to hold because they are able to get away so quickly. These little pets need gentle handling. Gerbils also prefer quiet voices; screaming and yelling startles them.

FERRETS

Ferrets sleep a lot, but they are curious, playful, and very active when they are awake.

A pet ferret needs to be let out of its cage for a while every day to keep from getting bored. While it is out, a ferret should be watched very closely. This mischievous pet explores everything, and it can get into trouble when it is loose in the house.

But a word of warning: A ferret doesn't always make the best pet. It can be a bit stinky. Its body makes a smelly oil that the ferret rubs on things to mark its home territory. Also, a startled ferret might bite, and it has sharp teeth.

Ferrets are **RELATED** to **WEASELS,** otters, and **BADGERS.**

HORSES

A horse can be a wonderful pet. But it is not one that can come in your house and snuggle up with you on the couch! Horses live outside.

Some horses are kept mainly to help with work on ranches and farms. But other horses are kept just for fun, as pets. People who have horses enjoy riding them. To ride a horse safely, both the horse and the rider need special gear, like that shown here. The horse's equipment is called tack.

BASIC NEEDS

safe, fenced pasture

clean water

fresh grass or hay, grain

shelter, such as a barn

The **HELMET** protects the rider's head in case she falls off.

Always approach a **HORSE** from the **SIDE,** where it can see you and **WON'T GET STARTLED.**

The rider sits in the **SADDLE** to ride.

The **SADDLE PAD** lies on the horse's back. It keeps the horse comfortable underneath the saddle.

RIDING BOOTS help keep the rider's feet in the stirrups.

The rider holds the **REINS** to guide the horse.

Part of the **BRIDLE,** called the bit, goes into the horse's mouth. The rest of the bridle fits over the horse's head.

The **GIRTH** is a belt attached to the saddle. It goes around the horse's belly.

The rider's feet go into the **STIRRUPS** on each side of the horse.

95

SHETLAND PONIES

A pony is a small horse. There are many breeds of ponies. One of the most popular breeds is the Shetland pony.

Horse and pony **HEIGHT** is measured at their **WITHERS**. That is the **SPOT** where the neck begins above the **SHOULDERS**.

The size of a regular horse can be a little scary when you are just beginning to learn how to ride. So kids often learn how to ride horses by starting out on a Shetland pony.

If you were learning to ride, would you rather start on a pony or a horse? Why?

LET'S PLAY A GAME!

A pattern is something that repeats. The pets make a different pattern in each row in this game. Can you say which pet comes next in the pattern in each row?

2 HARDER

RAT · FERRET · GERBIL · RAT · FERRET

3 HARDEST

RABBIT · GUINEA PIG · RABBIT · HAMSTER · RABBIT

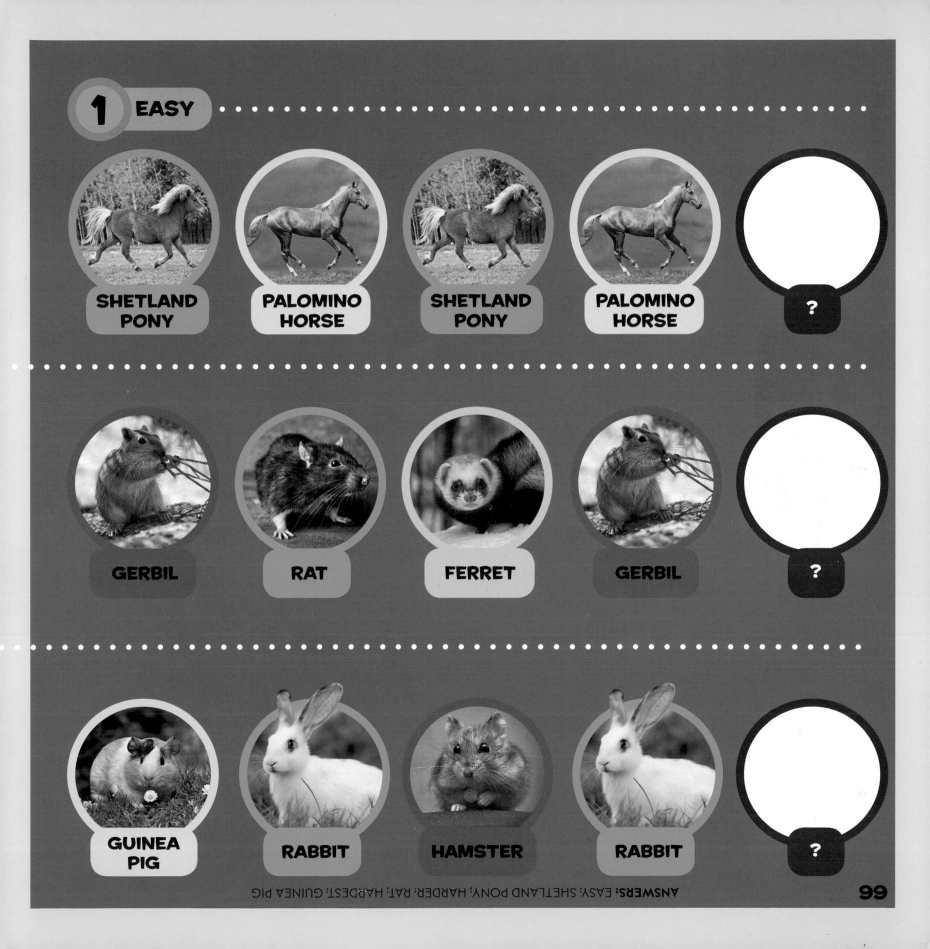

SHETLAND PONY

PALOMINO HORSE

SHETLAND PONY

PALOMINO HORSE

?

GERBIL

RAT

FERRET

GERBIL

?

GUINEA PIG

RABBIT

HAMSTER

RABBIT

?

ANSWERS: EASY: SHETLAND PONY, HARDER: RAT, HARDEST: GUINEA PIG

In this chapter you will discover pets with feathers, pets with scales, pets that fly, and pets that swim.

COCKATIELS

A pet **COCKATIEL** may **LIVE 25 YEARS.**

BASIC NEEDS

cage with perches

company: its human family or another cockatiel

cockatiel pellets, fresh fruit and vegetable seeds

fresh water

small bird toys

Look up in the trees when you take a walk, and you will probably see birds. Cardinals, blue jays, sparrows, and more fly around wild outside.

TOYS FOR PET COCKATIELS

- Chew toys to gnaw on
- Rope toys
- Pocket toys for hiding food
- Shredding toys for fun ripping
- Cuddle toy to nest in
- Swings and ladders for exercise

A cockatiel is startled by **LOUD NOISES.** It prefers **GENTLE HANDLING** and **HUSHED VOICES.**

A few kinds of birds are domesticated and make good pets. One of these is the cockatiel. Cockatiels are great whistlers. They often imitate, or copy, people who whistle a tune. They can learn to whistle a whole song. Some male cockatiels can even learn how to say words!

Can you think of any other toys a cockatiel might like to play with?

BUDGERIGARS AND LOVEBIRDS

Budgerigars, called budgies for short, and lovebirds also make good pets. Budgies are small parakeets. Lovebirds are small parrots.

Budgies come in a variety of colors, including blue and violet. Some budgies can be taught to say words, while others will only whistle.

BUDGIES

BASIC NEEDS

small-bird food from pet store

millet (a treat for birds)

a cage big enough for the bird to spread its wings and fly across

toys such as mirrors, ladders, bells, and swings

LOVEBIRDS

LOVEBIRDS might **BITE,** especially if **STARTLED.** If your lovebird **NIPS** you, give it a **TIME-OUT** in its cage.

Lovebirds are smart little birds that can learn tricks. They are friendly and like to cuddle. It is a good idea to get two lovebirds or two budgies, so that they can keep each other company when you are not around. To keep budgies or lovebirds from getting bored, add some bird toys to their cage.

MORE PET BIRDS

Zebra finches and society finches make good pet birds and are easy to take care of. Finches are tiny birds. The zebra finch is quiet. Society finches sing and chirp a lot. Finches need to live with other finches.

ZEBRA FINCHES

RING-NECKED DOVES

CANARY

Two kinds of doves make popular pets: the diamond dove and the ring-necked dove. Both kinds make soft cooing sounds that many people enjoy. These birds need the company of other birds or their human family.

Canaries are known for their beautiful singing. Males sing more than females. These birds are not fond of being held. They would rather be left in their cages. Canaries do not mind living in their cages alone. They come in many colors, including yellow, orange, red, brown, black, and white.

What are some words that describe the birds you see when you are outside?

CORN SNAKES AND MILK SNAKES

A **CORN SNAKE** can grow to **SIX FEET** (1.8 m) long.

CORN SNAKE

Snakes are reptiles, a group of animals generally covered with dry scales. Lizards, crocodiles, and turtles are also reptiles. Some species of snakes make interesting pets, but there are important things to think about before getting one.

BASIC NEEDS

terrarium with fastened screen top

mice to eat

water to drink

places to hide inside the terrarium

bedding, such as newspaper, for bottom of tank

First of all, pet snakes don't eat their food out of a bowl like a dog, cat, or hamster. These snakes need to be fed mice, which you can buy at a pet store. Also, it takes patience to get a snake comfortable with gentle handling.

If your family decides to get a pet snake, a milk snake or a corn snake is a good choice. The milk snake has three colors—usually red, black, and yellow—arranged in bands around its body. It is a calm snake. The more you handle it, the tamer it is likely to become.

A corn snake is colorful, too. It generally has red splotches on its back and a black-and-white checkered pattern on its belly.

PYTHONS, BOA CONSTRICTORS, and **ANACONDAS** do not make good pets. They may start out small, but they grow to be very **LARGE** and **DANGEROUS.**

MILK SNAKE

A **MILK SNAKE** can grow to **SEVEN FEET** (2 m) long.

LIZARDS, TURTLES, AND FROGS

Besides snakes, some people keep other reptiles, such as lizards and turtles, as pets. Some people keep amphibians, such as frogs and salamanders, as pets.

But like snakes, these animals need special care that can be hard to provide. They need just the right environment—including temperature, humidity (the amount of moisture in the air), and lighting—to stay healthy. They need special diets.

Probably, at least until you are an adult, these animals are best enjoyed in the wild, at zoos, and in photographs like these.

RED-EARED SLIDER

EASTERN BOX TURTLE

110

BEARDED DRAGON

LEOPARD GECKO

DWARF CLAWED FROG

WASH THOSE HANDS

Snakes and other reptiles and frogs and other amphibians all carry a kind of bacteria called salmonella inside them. Salmonella can make people sick. So it is very important to wash your hands thoroughly after handling a reptile or amphibian.

WHITE'S TREE FROG

111

HERMIT CRABS

Digging in sand and climbing rocks is all the exercise a hermit crab needs. This little creature is a crustacean, a group of animals that includes crabs and lobsters. A hermit crab is an easy pet to take care of—and fun to watch. Set up a terrarium, or clear glass tank, with sand, rocks, freshwater and salt water, and hiding places. Then add a couple of hermit crabs and let the fun begin!

Hermit crabs use abandoned snail shells for shelter. They carry their shells wherever they go. As they grow, they search for

BASIC NEEDS

hermit crab pellets

freshwater

salt water (made with special aquarium salt, not table salt)

fresh fruit and vegetables as a treat

terrarium with a warm temperature of about 75°F (24°C)

rocks and sand

daily misting with water to keep terrarium humid

places to hide and climb

new, larger shells for growing pet

A hermit crab has **FIVE PAIRS OF LEGS.** It uses two pairs for walking, one pair for eating and climbing, one pair for fighting and climbing, and one pair to hold on to its shell.

What are some new things that you need as you grow bigger?

Hermit **CRABS** can go a **WEEK WITHOUT EATING.**

To pick up your **PET CRAB,** hold its shell in one hand and place its legs on the **FLAT PALM** of your other hand. He is less likely to pinch this way.

larger shells to use. When they find the right size, they crawl from the small shell to the bigger one and make themselves at home. If you have a pet hermit crab, you'll need to provide it with bigger and bigger shells as it grows.

113

GOLDFISH

BASIC NEEDS

aquarium (fish bowl or tank)

goldfish food: flakes and pellets

cool, clean water to live in

Beautiful goldfish make great fishy pets. Goldfish are quite easy to keep. To stay healthy, they need a clean home. While a goldfish can do okay in a fish bowl, a larger aquarium is even better.

It is fun to decorate your fish tank for your goldfish. From toy castles and dragons to rocks and plants, you can use your imagination to create a special home for your fish.

How would you decorate a fish tank for goldfish?

GOLDFISH COME IN ALL SORTS OF SHAPES, SIZES, AND COLORS. HERE ARE JUST A FEW.

FANTAIL

VEILTAIL

TELESCOPE

BLACK MOOR

LIONHEAD

ORANDA

CELESTIAL

BUBBLE EYE

RYUKIN

BETTAS

Bettas are also called Siamese fighting fish. These fish can live with other species, but not with their own kind. Male bettas fight each other if there are two in a tank. Females might share a tank peacefully, but not always.

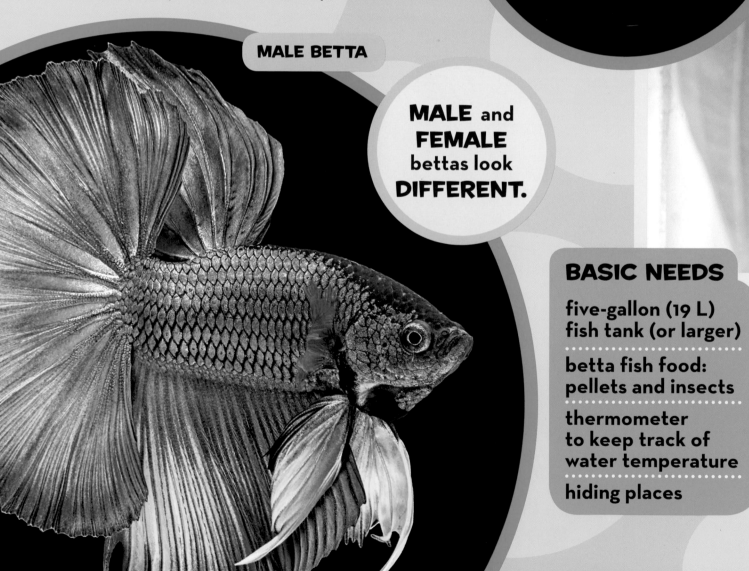

FEMALE BETTA

MALE BETTA

MALE and **FEMALE** bettas look **DIFFERENT.**

BASIC NEEDS

five-gallon (19 L) fish tank (or larger)

betta fish food: pellets and insects

thermometer to keep track of water temperature

hiding places

Bettas live **TWO** to **FOUR YEARS.**

BETTAS like their **WATER WARM.**

Where do you like to swim?

Most fish breathe through gills. Gills take in oxygen from the water. Bettas are a kind of labyrinth (LAH-buh-rinth) fish. These fish have gills, but they also have a special body part called a labyrinth. It lets the fish breathe when it is out of the water. A pet betta often swims to the surface of its tank and breathes air.

MIXED FISH TANK

A fish tank filled with several different kinds of fish gives a family a lot of pets! Some fish, like bettas, like warm water. Other species, such as goldfish, prefer cold water.

What would you like best about having a big fish tank?

Here are some examples of fish that live well together in warm tanks or cold tanks. A pet store worker can help your family pick out even more.

WARM WATER AQUARIUM

PEARL DANIO

GREEN SWORDTAIL

MICKEY MOUSE PLATY

BANDIT CORY CATFISH

COLD WATER AQUARIUM

BLOODFIN TETRA

WHITE CLOUD

ZEBRA DANIO

LET'S PLAY A GAME!

Help the five kids find their way to the pet they want to take home. Follow the correct path with your finger.

COCKATIELS

CORN SNAKE

GOLDFISH

HERMIT CRAB

LOVEBIRDS

PARENT TIPS

Extend your child's experience beyond the pages of this book. If you have a pet, you already have a great start. If you do not yet have a pet, there are several ways to introduce your child to the joys and responsibilities of having one. Taking your little one with you as you pet-sit for friends who need someone to feed their cat or walk their dog, and visiting a local animal shelter to see the pets available for adoption are great ways to continue satisfying your child's curiosity about pets. Here are some other activities you can do with National Geographic's *Little Kids First Big Book of Pets*.

BAKE DOG BISCUITS (COOKING)

Help your child make these simple dog treats for your own dog or a friend's dog.

INGREDIENTS:
• 2½ cups (320 g) whole wheat or all-purpose flour
• 1 teaspoon (5 mL) salt
• 1 egg
• ½ cup (250 mL) beef or chicken broth
• bacon bits and/or shredded cheese, for flavor

DIRECTIONS:
• Preheat oven to 350°F (180°C).
• Mix all ingredients together in a bowl.
• Knead dough for about three minutes, until it can be shaped into a ball.
• Roll out dough to ½-inch (1-cm) thick.
• Use cookie cutters to make shapes.
• Place shapes onto a lightly greased cookie sheet.
• Bake for 30 minutes.

20 QUESTIONS (DEDUCTION)

Play 20 questions with your child, using pets as the theme. Have your child think of a pet first. Ask her "yes" or "no" questions to figure out what kind of pet or pet-related object she is thinking of. If you ask her 20 questions without guessing correctly, she wins. Change roles. Make the game as specific as appropriate— "dog" or "German shepherd," "fish" or "aquarium," "horse" or "saddle."

PET JOKES (HUMOR)

Kids enjoy goofy jokes, funny riddles, and silly word play. Find pet jokes online and in joke books, or make up your own. Encourage your child to make up his own, too. Here are a couple of riddles to get you started.

Q. What do you get when you cross a cat with a parrot?
A. A CARROT!

Q. Why did the dog stay in the shade?
A. SO HE WOULDN'T TURN INTO A HOT DOG!

CREATE A PET POSTER
(ARTS AND CRAFTS)

Suggest that your child create a "Pets Poster" to hang in her bedroom or to give someone as a gift. Help your child cut out pictures of pets from magazines, catalogs, and newspapers. Provide her with poster board, crayons, markers, and glue sticks, along with craft store items such as stickers, felt, and feathers, and let her creativity take over.

SING SONGS
(MUSIC)

Sing songs about pets with your child. "How Much Is That Doggie in the Window" and "B-I-N-G-O" are a couple of examples. Look for these and other pet-themed songs online and learn them together. Encourage your child to make up his own lyrics and tunes. Add in drums, tambourines, or other instruments for more musical fun.

GO FISH GAME
(STRATEGY)

Teach your child the card game "Go Fish." Each player starts with five cards. Take turns asking a player of choice for a specific card. If you are asked for a three, for example, and you have any, you give all your threes to the player asking. If you do not, you say "Go fish!" That player picks up a card from the main deck. If the player gets the card she asked for, she gets another turn. Whenever someone has four cards of a kind, those cards are taken out of play and the player gets a point. If a player runs out of cards while there are still cards left in the deck, she gets five new cards. The game is over when no one has any cards left and the main deck is gone. The winner is the one with the most points.

GLOSSARY

AMPHIBIANS
a group of animals that includes frogs, toads, salamanders, and newts

AQUARIUM
a tank of water, usually made of glass, where fish and other water animals live in captivity

BACTERIA
tiny living things too small to see without a microscope

BREED
a group of animals within a species that are developed by humans to look the same, such as German shepherds

BREEDER
a person who raises animals

DOMESTIC ANIMAL
a kind of animal that people have tamed over a long period of time and that is very different from its ancestors in the wild

EQUINE VETERINARIAN
a medical doctor who specializes in the care of horses

FERAL
a domesticated animal that never lives with humans

LIVESTOCK
farm animals raised mainly for food, such as cows, sheep, goats, and pigs

MAMMALS
a group of animals with backbones, including humans, that are warm-blooded, breathe air, have hair, and nurse their young

PET
an animal that lives with people and keeps them company

PUREBRED

an animal that is one breed within its species

REPTILES

a group of animals that includes snakes, turtles, lizards, and crocodiles

STRAY

a lost pet

TAME ANIMAL

a wild animal that has become used to people and is unafraid around them

TERRARIUM

an enclosure, usually made of glass, for small land animals

VETERINARIAN

a medical doctor for animals

ADDITIONAL RESOURCES

BOOKS

National Geographic Kids. *Just Joking Cats*. National Geographic Kids Books, 2016.

Newman, Aline Alexander, and Gary Weitzman. *How to Speak Cat: A Guide to Decoding Cat Language*. National Geographic Kids Books, 2015.

Newman, Aline Alexander, and Gary Weitzman. *How to Speak Dog: A Guide to Decoding Dog Language*. National Geographic Kids Books, 2013.

Spears, James. *Everything Pets*. National Geographic Kids Books, 2013.

WEBSITES

animalhumanesociety.org
cdc.gov/healthypets/pets/index.html
akc.org
cfa.org/Breeds.aspx

INDEX

Photo Credits

AL = Alamy; DS = Dreamstime; GI = Getty Images; IS = iStock; MP = Minden Pictures; SS = Shutterstock; TS = Thinkstock

Cover (CTR RT), tea maeklong/SS; (LO RT), Zurijeta/SS; (LO CTR), Hira Punjabi/AL; (LO LE), dageldog/GI; (CTR LE), Image Source/AL; (UP LE), Gunnar Pippel/SS; (UP RT), Wildlife GmbH/AL; (UP RT), Oksana Kuzmina/SS; spine, Oktay Ortakcioglu/IS; back cover: (UP), Ermolaev Alexander/SS; (LO), vovan/SS; 1, S-F/SS; 2–3, Image Source/GI; 4 (UP), cynoclub/SS; 4 (LO LE, LO RT), Eric Isselee/SS; 5 (UP), Intherayoflight/SS; 5 (CTR), Twin Design/SS; 5 (LO), Stephaniellen/SS; 8–9, warrengoldswain/TS; 10 (UP), ESB Professional/SS; 11 (UP LE), Samuel Borges Photography/SS; 11 (UP RT, LO CTR LE, CTR RT), Eric Isselee/SS; 11 (CTR UP LE), Marco Govel/IS; 11 (gray cat), Jagodka/SS; 11 (striped cat), Steve Heap/SS; 11 (CTR LE), Rebecca Hale/NG Staff; 11 (CTR LO LE), Rebecca Hale/NG Staff; 11 (LO LE), Yuri Arcurs/SS; 11 (LO CTR RT), MirasWonderland/SS; 11 (LO RT), Pakula Piotr/SS; 11 (CTR RT), Eric Isselee/DS; 12–13 (RT), Holly Kuchera/SS; 13 (UP), EcoPrint/SS; 13 (LO RT), Stubblefieldphoto/DS; 14, MPH Photos/SS; 15 (UP), Dzurag/TS; 16 (UP), The Len/SS; 17 (LO), Daniel Prudek/SS; 17 (UP), Anke Van Wyk/DS; 18 (LO), MonumentalDoom/IS/GI; 18–19 (CTR), FatCamer/IS/GI; 20 (LO), Nomad_Soul/SS; 20 (UP), onetouchspark/IS/GI; 21, Photo by Laurie Cinotto/GI; 22 (LO), DjelicS/GI; 22–23, kali9/GI; 24 (LO LE, LO RT), Juan Silva/GI; 24–25 (UP), hedgehog94/SS; 26 (UP LE), vovan/SS; 26 (UP CTR, LO RT), Eric Isselee/DS; 26 (UP RT), Eric Isselee/SS; 26 (LO LE), IrinaK/SS; 26 (LO CTR), Tsekhmister/SS; 27 (UP LE, CTR), Eric Isselee/SS; 27 (UP CTR), Eric Isselee/DS; 27 (UP RT), Tiger/IS; 27 (LO LE), James Pierce/SS; 27 (LO CTR), Erik Lam/SS; 28–29, Johny87/GI; 30 (UP), Orientgold/SS; 30 (CTR), Africa Studio/SS; 30 (LO), hd connelly/SS; 31 (UP), Jim Craigmyle/GI; 32 (LE), Danita Delimont/GI; 32 (RT), Eric Isselee/SS; 33 (LO CTR), Cynoclub/DS; 33 (UP), Aline Alexander Newman; 33 (LO LE), PardoY/SS; 33 (LO RT), Nature Picture Library/AL; 34 (LO RT, LO RT), schubbel/SS; 34 (UP LE, LO LE), Eric Isselee/SS; 34 (UP RT), Kuznetsov Alexey/SS; 35 (UP RT), Erik Lam/SS; 35 (CTR RT), Tatyana Kuznetsova/SS; 35 (UP LE), Julia_Siomuha/TS; 35 (LO LE), Eric Isselee/SS; 35 (LO RT), Liliya Kulianionak/SS; 35 (CTR LE), IS/TS; 36 (LO LE), Dennis Jacobsen/DS; 36 (LO RT), Jagodka/SS; 36 (UP LE), NORRIE3699/SS; 36 (UP RT), Eve Photography/SS; 37 (CTR LE), kimrawicz/TS; 37 (UP CTR), CaptureLight/TS; 37 (UP LE), Vicente Barcelo Varona/SS; 37 (CTR), KaliAntye/SS; 37 (LO LE), chaoss/SS; 37 (UP RT), volofin/SS; 37 (LO RT), Dorottya Mathe/SS; 37 (LO CTR), everydoghasastory/SS; 38 (LE), otsphoto/SS; 38 (RT), Nuttapong/SS; 38–39 (CTR RT), Stephen Simpson/GI; 39 (LO RT), Clarissa Leahy/GI; 40–41 (UP CTR), Lori Epstein; 40 (LO), goodluz/SS; 41 (UP), Monkey Business Images/SS; 42–43 (CTR), Debra Bardowicks/GI; 43 (LO), Adi Wong/EyeEm/GI; 44 (LO), Dan Kosmayer/SS; 44 (UP), Daniel Teetor/AL Stock Photo; 45 (CTR LE), Fayzulin Serg/SS; 45 (UP), Image by Ian Carroll (aka "icypics")/GI; 45 (CTR RT), Photographer Nick Measures/GI; 45 (LO), jurgisr/IS/GI; 46–47 (CTR RT), Golden Pixels LLC/SS; 47 (UP), eurobanks/SS; 48–49 (CTR), Cultura Motion/SS; 49 (UP), art nick/SS; 49 (LO LE), Bulltus_casso/SS; 49 (LO RT), BW Folsom/SS; 50 (UP), Bigandt_Photography/IS; 51 (RT), Jupiterimages/TS; 51 (LO), Djent/SS; 52 (dog), Dorottya Mathe/SS; 52 (CTR LE), Paul Michael Hughes/SS; 52 (LO LE), antpkr/SS; 52 (LO CTR), lammotos/SS; 52 (LO RT), Anna Hoychuk/SS; 53 (UP LE), By Anurak Pongpatimet/SS; 53 (UP RT), hd connelly/SS; 53 (CTR RT, CTR, LO), cynoclub/SS; 53 (CTR LE), Paul Michael Hughes/SS; 54–55, Photo-SD/SS; 56 (UP), Fotosearch/GI; 57 (UP), Martin Ruegner/GI; 57 (CTR), Africa Studio/SS; 57 (LO), Bulltus_casso/SS; 58 (UP), Giedriius/SS; 58 (LO LE), By Hannamariah/SS; 58 (LO RT), Katrina Brown/AL Stock Photo; 59, Sari O'Neal/AL; 60 (UP LE), Rika-sama/SS; 60 (UP RT), Tine Robbe/SS; 60 (LO LE), Benjamin B/SS; 60 (LO CTR), cath5/SS; 60 (LO RT), fantom_rd/SS; 60 (UP CTR), Jupiterimages/GI; 61 (CTR LE), Vadim Petrakov/SS; 61 (CTR RT), Eric Isselee/SS; 61 (LO), Elisa Putti/SS; 61 (UP RT), Photography Selfmade/SS; 61 (UP LE), alexavol/SS; 62 (LO RT), kenez/SS; 62 (UP LE), nelik/SS; 62 (UP RT), Viktor Sergeevich/SS; 62 (LO CTR), Alex Farias/SS; 62 (UP CTR), imageBROKER/AL; 62 (LO LE), MJ Photography/AL; 62 (UP RT), mauritius images GmbH/AL; 63 (UP LE), DragoNika/SS; 63 (CTR LE), otsphoto/SS; 63 (CTR RT), Eric Isselee/SS; 63 (CTR), Cristina Annibali/SS; 63 (LO RT), jojosmb/SS; 63 (LO LE), Voraorn Ratanakorn/SS; 64 (UP), Benjamin Torode/GI; 64 (LO), Hurst Photo/SS; 65 (UP), GK Hart/Vikki Hart/GI; 65 (LO), Casey Elise Christopher/SS; 66–67 (CTR), Kasefoto/SS; 66 (LO), Alena Ozerova/SS; 67 (LO), traumlichtfabrik/GI; 68 (UP), Andreykuzmin/DS; 68 (LO), Anurak Pongpatimet/SS; 69 (LO LE), Christine Widdall/AL; 69 (UP RT), Annaav/SS; 69 (UP LE), Tycson1/SS; 69 (LO RT), Krissi Lundgren/SS; 71 (LO RT), Veera/SS; 72–73/SS; 73 (UP), Africa Studio/SS; 73 (UP), Chendongshan/SS; 74 (LO), Maria Sauh/SS; 75 (UP), Alena Ozerova/SS; 75 (LO), Chendongshan/SS; 76–77 (LO LE), w-ings/IS/GI; 77 (LO), Tracy Morgan/GI; 78 (cat), 5 second Studio/SS; 78 (polaroid frame), Nelson Marques/SS; 78 (polaroid frames), Nelson Marques/SS; 79 (polaroid frames), Nelson Marques/SS; 79 (UP LE), Geoffrey Jones/SS; 79 (CTR RT), Grigorita Ko/SS; 79 (UP RT), Yuryi Oleinikov/SS; 79 (CTR LE), By Photocreo Michal Bednarek/SS; 79 (LO CTR), Casey Elise Christopher/SS; 79 (LO RT), Andrey Denisenkov/SS; 79 (LO LE), cynoclub/SS; 80–81, Juta/SS; 82 (UP), Tierfotoagentur/ALStockPhoto; 82 (LO), 5 second Studio/SS; 83 (UP), Tierfotoagentur/R. Richter/age fotostock; 83 (LO), gary vanfleet/GI; 84 (UP RT), Linn Currie/SS; 84 (LO RT), Cora Mueller/SS; 84 (UP LE), Georgia Evans/DS; 84 (LO LE), Lynn Stone/GI; 84 (LO CTR), adogslifephoto/TS; 85 (UP CTR), Tom Karola/SS; 85 (UP RT), Mualchon Chartsuwan/SS; 85 (LO RT), cynoclub/SS; 85 (LO LE), Angela Hampton/MP; 85 (UP LE), Shannon Hibberd/NG STAFF; 86 (UP), Zoonar GmbH/AL; 86 (CTR), Bulltus_casso/SS; 87 (UP LE), Lynn Stone/GI; 87 (LO RT), Seregraff/SS; 87 (LO LE), Chorch/SS; 87 (UP RT), Tettania/SS; 88, stock_shot/SS; 89 (LO RT), Clari Massimiliano/SS; 89 (UP RT), retales botijero/GI; 90 (CTR), Skachkova/SS; 91 (LO), Anna Hoychuk/SS; 91 (UP), Juniors Bildarchiv GmbH/AL; 92 (UP), Bildagentur Zoonar GmbH/SS; 93 (LO), Couperfield/SS; 94–95, Adie Bush/GI; 96 (UP), Bob Langrish/GI; 96 (LO), Grigorita Ko/SS; 97 (BACKGROUND), cynoclub/SS; 98 (UP LE, UP CTR RT, CTR CTR LE), Africa Studio/SS; 98 (UP CTR LE, UP RT), vainer/SS; 98 (UP CTR), Yerbolat Shadrakhov/SS; 98 (LO CTR LE), Miroslav Hlavko/SS; 98 (LO CTR RT), Sahan Svitlana/SS; 98 (LO LE, LO CTR, LO RT), Byrdyak/IS; 99 (UP LE), Miroslav Hlavko/SS; 99 (CTR LE, CTR RT), Yerbolat Shadrakhov/SS; 99 (CTR CTR RT), vainer/SS; 99 (LO CTR RT), Sahan Svitlana/SS; 99 (UP LE, UP CTR RT), Grigorita Ko/SS; 99 (UP CTR LE, UP RT), mariait/SS; 99 (LO CTR LE, LO RT), Byrdyak/IS; 100–101, PixieMe/SS; 102 (UP), Butterfly Hunter/SS; 103 (UP), Nipa Noymol/SS; 103 (LO), Kyli Petersen/SS; 105–106 (CTR), apichon_tee/SS; 104 (LO), Matthew Cuda/AL; 105 (UP), Andrii Shevchuk/DS; 106 (LO), Empiric7/SS; 107 (UP LE), Paul Broadbent/SS; 107 (UP RT), Jana Mackova/SS; 108 (UP), Ryan Ladbrook/SS; 109 (LO), amwu/TS; 110 (LO), Ryan M. Bolton/SS; 110 (UP), Ivan Kuzmin/AL Stock Photo; 111 (UP LE), Robert Keresztes/SS; 111 (UP RT), By MZPHOTO.CZ/SS; 111 (CTR LE), Milan Zygmunt/SS; 111 (LO), blickwinkel/AL Stock Photo; 111 (CTR RT), LooksLikeLisa/SS; 112–113 (UP), HIRA PUNJABI/AL Stock Photo; 113 (LO), Shinji Kusano/MP; 114 (UP), dien/SS; 115 (UP LE), Sergey Lavrentev/SS; 115 (CTR LE), leisuretime70/SS; 115 (CTR, UP RT), bluehand/SS; 115 (CTR RT), dien/SS; 115 (LO CTR), Arunee Rodloy/SS; 115 (LO LE), 9george/SS; 115 (LO UP CTR), skydie/SS; 115 (LO RT), Pindiyath100/SS; 116 (LO), Wataru Utada/SS; 116–117, surachet khamsuk/SS; 116–117, picstyle99/IS/GI; 118 (LO), tetiana_u/SS; 119 (UP RT), NERYXCOM/SS; 119 (LO RT), Kazakov Maksim/SS; 119 (LO LE), Grigorev Mikhail/SS; 119 (UP CTR LE), Lucky Business/SS; 119 (UP CTR RT), Paulo Oliveira/AL Stock Photo; 119 (UP CTR RT), Arco Images GmbH/AL Stock Photo; 119 (UP LE), Copora/DS; 120 (UP LE), Stephaniellen/SS; 120 (UP CTR), Kamira/SS; 120 (UP RT), leungchopan/SS; 120 (LO), Enrique Ramos/SS; 121 (UP LE), dien/SS; 121 (UP RT), Vol. Kozin/SS; 121 (CTR LE), DenisNata/SS; 121 (LO RT), Hogan Imaging/SS; 121 (CTR RT), gillmar/SS; 121 (LO LE), tea maeklong/SS; 122 (UP), Vladyslav Starozhylov/SS; 123 (LO), Jacobs Stock Photography Ltd/GI; 124 (UP), Squamish/IS/GI; 124 (LO), Eric Isselee/SS; 125 (LO), Masahiro Suzuki/SS; 128 (RT), Eric Isselee/SS

For Alexandra, Andrew, and Samuel,
who each have a very special place in my heart.
—Cee Cee

Since 1888, the National Geographic Society has funded more than 12,000 research, exploration, and preservation projects around the world. The Society receives funds from National Geographic Partners, LLC, funded in part by your purchase. A portion of the proceeds from this book supports this vital work. To learn more, visit natgeo.com/info.

NATIONAL GEOGRAPHIC and Yellow Border Design are trademarks of the National Geographic Society, used under license.

For more information, visit nationalgeographic.com, call 1-800-647-5463, or write to the following address:
National Geographic Partners
1145 17th Street N.W.
Washington, D.C. 20036-4688 U.S.A.

Visit us online at nationalgeographic.com/books

For librarians and teachers: ngchildrensbooks.org

More for kids from National Geographic: natgeokids.com

National Geographic Kids magazine inspires children to explore their world with fun yet educational articles on animals, science, nature, and more. Using fresh storytelling and amazing photography, Nat Geo Kids shows kids ages 6 to 14 the fascinating truth about the world—and why they should care. **kids.nationalgeographic.com/subscribe**

For information about special discounts for bulk purchases, please contact National Geographic Books Special Sales: specialsales@natgeo.com

For rights or permissions inquiries, please contact National Geographic Books Subsidiary Rights: bookrights@natgeo.com

Designed by Nicole Lazarus, Design Superette

Library of Congress Cataloging-in-Publication Data
Names: Hughes, Catherine D., author. | National Geographic Kids (Firm), publisher. | National Geographic Society (U.S.)
Title: Little kids first big book of pets / by Catherine D. Hughes.
Other titles: First big book of pets
Description: Washington, DC : National Geographic Kids, [2019] | Series: Little kids first big book | Audience: Ages 4-8. | Audience: K to grade 3.
Identifiers: LCCN 2018035847 (print) | LCCN 2018039022 (ebook) | ISBN 9781426334726 (e-book) | ISBN 9781426334702 (hardcover) | ISBN 9781426334719 (hardcover)
Subjects: LCSH: Pets--Juvenile literature.
Classification: LCC SF416.2 (ebook) | LCC SF416.2 .H84 2019 (print) | DDC 636.088/7--dc23
LC record available at https://lccn.loc.gov/2018035847

The publisher would like to acknowledge and thank Dr. Carol Osborne, DVM, and early childhood learning specialist Barbara Bradley for their expert insights and guidance. Many thanks also to project manager Grace Hill Smith and researcher Sharon Thompson for their invaluable help with this book.

Printed in China
19/PPS/1